Keep What God Gives
John Osteen

Jesus said in John 10:10: "The thief cometh not, but for to steal, and to kill, and to destroy: **I am come that they might have life, and that they might have it more abundantly.**"

The Bible also says, "Christ has redeemed us from the curse of the law, being made a curse for us. For it is written cursed is everyone that hangeth on a tree, that the blessings of Abraham might come on the Gentiles through Jesus Christ..." (Galatians 3:13-14).

God *wants* us to be a blessed people. As a good Father, He *wants* to give us good things to enjoy in this life. Now I realize that many of us have already received the good things that God has given.

He has given us health.
He has given us strength.

He has given us prosperity.

He has given us healing — mental, emotional and physical healing. He has blessed us with wonderful families, and many other things that we rejoice in.

Did you know, however, that there is an enemy that will steal and destroy all that God has given you?

Many of you who are reading this book have already lost many of the blessings of God. Many of you who are reading these lines are in danger of losing some of the blessings of God. My desire is to help you.

Three Things the Devil Wants to Do

I want you to know that you do have an enemy. That enemy is the devil. I am going to give you three passages of scripture that tell you three things that the devil is intent on doing to you if you remain ignorant of his devices.

The first scripture is found in Matthew 12:43-45: "When the unclean spirit is gone out of a man, he walketh through dry places, seeking rest, and findeth none. Then he saith, I will return into my house from whence I came out; and when he is come, he findeth it empty, swept, and garnished. Then goeth he, and taketh with himself seven other spirits more wicked than himself, and they enter in and dwell there; and the last state of that man is worse than the first."

John 10:10: "The thief cometh not, but for to steal, and to kill, and to destroy: I am come that they might have life, and that they might have it more abundantly."

I Peter 5:8: "Be sober, be vigilant; because your adversary the devil, as a roaring lion, walketh about, seeking whom he may devour."

You will notice these scriptures tell us three things that the devil is determined to do. He said in the book of Matthew, I *will* return unto my house. He calls your body his house. He said, "I will *return*." In John 10:10 he said that he will *steal, kill,* and *destroy*. In I Peter 5:8 he says, "I will *devour*." These are three things the devil is determined to do.

I will return.

I will steal, kill and destroy.

I will devour.

This book is being written to help you know how to keep the devil from accomplishing his goal. I believe it is possible in these days to stand fast as more than a conqueror. I believe that God is going to help you as you read and meditate upon the truths written in this book.

I am a pastor. As a pastor, I teach the Bible to help people grow in the knowledge of God and learn their rights and privileges in Jesus Christ. As I write this book, I think of how privileged I am to be able to share the Word of God with hungry hearts.

I love you so much! I love the body of Christ. I count it a joy to share the good things of God.

It is a tragedy when men preach nonsense, unbelief, doubt and frivolity and waste people's precious time. What a responsibility we have to teach you something that will make you a stronger and a better Christian! As pastor of Lakewood Church in Houston, Texas, I continually ask myself after I preach, "Have I done any good? Did I feed anybody? Did I bless anybody? Did I really help the needy people who listened today?"

You see, at Lakewood Church we have great crowds of people that come to church. In the midst of the crowds are some who are ready to commit suicide. They are searching. They are desperate. In fact, there was a young man that came. He only visited there once. We didn't have enough time to help him. He went out and killed himself. After his death, I went into his home. I had never been there before. I didn't know the family. The boy had shot and killed himself. It was such a tragedy!

When people come to church, it is serious business. Some people are fighting for their very lives. Some of you may be reading this today just to enjoy it. Others of you need something from God to survive. You are struggling. Your cry is going up to God. You are searching.

I want to help you. My deepest desire is to inform God's people of the precious grace, mercy and knowledge of God. You need to know how to rise up in these last days with a personal knowledge of who you are in Christ and not have to depend on special personalities.

You can stand in the thick of the battle unwavering and unfaltering, with the Name of Jesus Christ, and send the devil fleeing in terror from you!!

It is important that you know how to keep what God has given you.

God has given many of you much. Many of you are enjoying the blessings of God. Many of you are enjoying wonderful health, financial prosperity, emotional stability, mental peace, and marital blessings.

Satan's Counter-Attack

I want you to know that you will not enjoy the blessings of God without being contested by your enemy.

More battles are lost and more blessings are lost on satan's *counter-attack* than any other time.

He will leave you alone for a while and suddenly he will make a *counter-attack* and surprise and alarm you. Many people lose what God has given them when satan makes his *counter-attack*. Many go back into poverty, emotional instability and mental torment. They say, "I thought God healed me. I thought I had the blessings of God. I thought God had visited me. It looks like I have lost it all."

You need to know how to keep what God has given you.

Why a Deaf Woman Lost Her Healing

I remember when I was ministering in Milwaukee, Wisconsin. I called for the deaf to be ministered for healing. A woman totally deaf came forward. She was not just partially deaf, but totally deaf in both ears. She came up on the platform along with others. We came against the deaf spirit, commanding it to go in Jesus' Name, and it left immediately. She then had perfect hearing.

She came back the next night and I saw her sitting there in the audience. When I gave the invitation for those who needed to be healed, someone with her urged her to come forward. She was totally deaf again. I cast out the deaf spirit again and she had perfect hearing instantly. She could hear anything.

On the third night, I saw her sitting out there and I noticed that she lifted her hand again indicating that she needed healing. She was sitting beside a man. I said to the pastor, "See that woman sitting out there beside her husband? She's totally deaf again."

He said, "Oh, Brother Osteen, don't be too concerned or alarmed about that! You see, that man that she's sitting by is not her husband. She is living with him in adultery, in open violation of God's law. The deaf demon does leave her every time you command it to go in Jesus' Name but the very minute she steps back in that house, that demon power has access to her and takes her hearing again. She is not going to change. You might as well just leave her alone. She has chosen her pathway."

So, she went out of the meeting that night and stayed deaf. You see, she lost her healing by giving place to the devil. The Bible says, "Give **no** place to the devil" (Ephesians 4:27). On the contrary, God says, "Resist the devil and he will flee from you" (James 4:7).

Did you know that you can lose your blessings by ignorance as well as sin?

Hosea 4:6 says: "My people are destroyed for lack of knowledge." What people need is not inspiration, they need information. Let's look at the Word of God and get Bible information that will help us.

In all three texts quoted at the beginning of this teaching, we have a revelation of three things the devil is determined to do. In Matthew 12:43, he said, *I will return*. The Lord Jesus revealed that it is the devil's stated purpose to come back against you. He wants to re-enter your life in some phase. He said, "I will return to my house."

He is too ignorant to know that your body is the temple of God. He still thinks it is *his house*. Ephesians 2:2-3 tells us that we once belonged to him. Ephesians 2:5 says that now we belong to God! "Even when we were dead in sins, hath quickened us together with Christ, (by grace ye are saved)."

I Corinthians 6:19-20: "What? Know ye not that your body is the temple of the Holy Ghost which is in you, which ye have of God, and ye are not your own?

"For ye are bought with a price: therefore glorify God in your body, and in your spirit, which are God's."

Can you imagine some demon talking with other demons about your precious body and calling it, "his house"?

He said, "I will return."

Now friends, I want you to know the devil is determined to return and try to take control of your life mentally, physically, financially, emotionally, and every other way. He is going to try to come back into your life in some area.

In John 10:10 it says that he is going to try to steal and to kill and to destroy. **Steal! Kill! Destroy!** These are revelation scriptures that tell you clearly the thoughts of satan, your enemy. The devil says, "I will steal what God has given you. I will kill you and your family. I will destroy your business and destroy your peace and destroy your happiness." Satan is an evil prince with demon forces under his command and he sends them forth to *steal, kill,* and *destroy.* Some people think they can just stick their head in the sand and ignore him and he will go away. No, he won't. He will come at you from every side. Just ignoring the devil does not send him away. He's determined to kill you. He is determined to steal everything he can from you. He is out to **destroy you.**

Don't Blame God!

As a pastor, I deal with lots of tragedies. People come to me brokenhearted and in tragedy. I hear them cry, **"Why has God done this to me?"**

They get mad at God.

Wouldn't it be refreshing for somebody to come to the pastor and say, **"Why has the devil done this to me? I'll never serve him. I'll never give in to him. He's a bad devil!"**

Instead, people get mad at God for what the devil does. The devil does it, and tells them that God did it. Somebody said, "Well, God killed my mother." He didn't kill your mother. "God killed my daddy." No, God didn't kill your daddy. "Well, God took my health." No, God never took your health. The devil is determined to steal not only your health, but to kill you! He wants to kill me. He wants to kill my wife. He wants to kill my children. But I have news for him, he's not going to do it! I know his purpose. He said, "I will return to my house." He says, "I will steal, I will kill, I will destroy."

First Peter 5:8 reads: "Be sober, be vigilant, because your adversary the devil, as a roaring lion, walketh about, seeking whom he may devour." The devil's purpose comes to light through this scripture also. He says, "I will devour."

Be sober! Be vigilant! Be on your toes! Be keen! Don't get apathetic or careless! Don't let your guard down!

Isn't it a tragedy that while the devil, our enemy, is so vigilant, so constant, so alert and so active that some of God's people are not alert and active, but would rather sit down and say, "Well I don't want the Word of God. I don't want to believe in the faith message. I don't want to be extreme. I don't want to trust the Bible. I don't want to get involved in all of that." They just want to "rock-a-bye-baby" in their little denominational cradle and go to bed early and not be so involved in all of these things. It's a reproach to the Name of Jesus!

If our enemy is so alert, we ought to be alert also! **Be sober, be vigilant!** Why? Because your adversary, your enemy, the devil walks about as a roaring lion, seeking whom **he may devour!**

Never have the devil and demon forces been more active than today. They have come forth in a mighty fury. They have made sons and daughters into homosexuals and lesbians. They have made husbands and wives into drunkards. They have broken up families. Preachers are seeing homes go down the drain all over this world. Men and women are feeling the assault and the attack of enemy forces. If there was ever a day when we needed truth, it is **today!**

Satan is out to do three things in order to take from you what God has given you.

I will return to my house!
I will steal, kill and destroy you!
I will devour you and your blessings!
Let's see what God tells us to do.

Hold Fast That Which You Already Have!

In Revelation 2:25 it says, *"Hold fast that which you already have."*

Some people think if God gave it to them, then it is forever theirs. Well it is, but somebody is going to try to steal it. The devil will try to take it from you. God says, *"Hold fast that which you already have!"* You already have it, so don't let the devil take it away. Stand your ground! Resist the devil! Hold fast to that which is yours!

I got on the plane one day and sat down. The man next to me pulled out a newspaper. I pulled out my Bible. I punched him in the ribs and said, "You have the bad news, I have the Good News!" I was underlining in the Bible. (I underline nearly everything in my Bible.) As I was reading my Bible and underlining, the man kept watching me in astonishment. He then said to me, "Why do you underline *everything?*" I said, "I just underline what is good." Thank God, all the Bible is good. You need to feed on the Word of God so you will know how to keep what God has given you. The Bible reveals your rights and privileges in Christ.

Some people say, "Well, I thought God healed me. I thought God gave me His blessing on my business and now it is failing and I am going bankrupt. Here I am feeling all the symptoms again. Here I am getting back in the same sad shape! I thought I was blessed!"

God says, **"Hold fast that which you already have!"** (Revelation 2:25)

Who is to hold fast?

You are!

The reason God tells you to hold fast is because there is a *force* that is going to seek to pull your blessings away from you. You are not going to keep your healing and you are not going to keep your blessings and you are not going to keep all the good things of God if you just lie down on your back and become lazy and let the devil slip up and take them away from you. The Bible says, *"Hold fast what you **already have!**"* Hold it fast!

In our church services we get our people to confess, "My house is paid for. My cars are paid for. All my bills are paid. I don't owe anybody anything. I have money in the bank. I am not stingy. I am not covetous. I am evangelizing the world." As a result, one by one our homes are getting paid off. I remember when ours was paid off, what a joyous day it was!

Now, what if I came home one day and some burly fellow was sitting in my debt-free house. What if he said to me, "Well, my family and I decided this is our new house." Would I just say, "Well I thought it was mine. Come on Dodie (my wife), come on children. We will have to get out." My wife would say, "No, let's don't leave. This is my house." I would say, "No, he says it's his. We will just have to leave." So, I gather my children, go out and just leave all because he said it was his.

Would I do that? **No! No! No!**

I would fight him "tooth and toenail!" I am not

going to work and pray and believe God to pay for my house just to have anybody, big or little, come in and take what is rightfully mine. I tell you, he would have a fight on his hands. I have a legal document that says it is mine! I have the title-deed!

Many Christians are not fighting for what is rightfully theirs. The devil comes around to steal everything and they just lie down. They roll over and act like it's his. You have a legal document — the Bible. Read it to the devil and command him in Jesus' Name to go!

Let me tell you a story about our dog, Scooter. I enjoy that dog. I used to ride a bicycle around our neighborhood. My dog, a big German shepherd, would trot along beside me. Scooter is so big and healthy-looking. I was so proud of that dog. He could "whip" a lion. He was strong and alert. He would run like a deer. I bragged on my dog everywhere I went.

One day I was riding along and a little tiny dog just about five inches high came running out at him. His legs were hardly bigger than matchsticks. As I watched him bark, I thought, "My dog, Scooter, is going to eat him up with one bite. Watch out! Goodbye little dog!" But that dog ran towards Scooter yapping and barking something mighty convincing in dog talk. He ran up to my big fine dog named Scooter, and my dog just turned over on his back, put up all four feet and gave up!

I wanted to kick him all the way home! I was so ashamed. Why he could have put one paw on that little dog and killed him! But he just rolled over and said, "I give up." I don't know what that little dog said in dog talk, but he was convincing!

Some people act just like my dog Scooter in the face of an attack. Some little, hairy demon no bigger than a rat runs out and starts yapping and telling them, "You are going to die. You have all the symptoms again. You are going to go broke. You are going to lose this and lose that." They just roll over and say, "Oh, my God, my God!" They tremble in fear. Then the devil just takes over.

No!
Stand up on your feet!
Use the Name of Jesus!

Hold fast that which you already have!

Don't give the devil one thing God has given you. It does not belong to him. You have a legal document. It is written down in the Word of God. This legal document says abundant life is yours.

Hold Fast Your Confession

What else does God tell us to do?

Hebrews 4:14 says: "Hold fast to your confession." Don't change your confession. Don't change your words. Don't begin to agree with what the devil tells you. Friends, if you begin to change what you say, you will lose it.

Hold fast to your confession.

How are you to hold on to what God has given you? How are you to do it? Renew your mind every day in the Word of God. Romans 12:2 says: "And be not conformed to this world: but be ye transformed by the renewing of your mind, that ye may prove what is that good, and acceptable, and perfect will of God."

Let God's Word live big in you.

Colossians 3:16: "Let the Word spoken by the Christ, the Messiah, have its home in your hearts and minds and dwell in you in all its richness..." (Amplified Bible). Live in the Word. Learn it until, like Jesus, you can say,"It is written," and whip the devil every time he attacks you.

Renew your mind in the Word of God. Think the thoughts of God, your Heavenly Father.

Curtis Bell was the Administrator of our church for many years before he went to Heaven. He was in charge of all our building programs. Years ago he was one of the first men in our church to receive the Baptism in the Holy Spirit. He had constantly suffered with allergies and hay fever. When the hay fever season began, he really suffered. This went on for many years before he received the Baptism in the Holy Spirit.

He learned of God's promise to heal, exercised faith in those promises, and God healed him *instantly!*

He went for years and years without one symptom. One day, many years later, he was in northeast Houston on his tractor plowing in ragweed. All at once, every symptom came back upon him. His eyes began to water. His nose began to run. Every symptom of hay fever came back on him. He was shocked. He stopped his tractor. He thought a minute. (Now if he'd been in some other church, I don't know what he would have done. Thank God, he had been under some good teaching. I'm not bragging on myself. I'm bragging on Jesus. I'm bragging on the Word of God.) He was startled for a moment and shocked. His first thought was, "My God, I thought I was healed; everything is back on me again."

Then the Word of God rose up within him! He bristled. He got angry. He said, "No you don't devil! No you don't devil! You're not going to put that back on me! **In the Name of Jesus, I command you, go!!**"

Every symptom left instantly. He never had

another symptom! He held fast to his confession of healing. He would not give up saying, "By His stripes I am healed!" He shouted in the face of the devil and all the symptoms!

You see, if he had accepted that hay fever again and said, "Well, I thought the message of healing was right, but it looks like it doesn't work in my case", that would have been just like signing for it. He would have been agreeing with the devil. Instead, he stood up and *held fast to his confession*. He agreed with God!

Curtis Bell **held fast to what God had already given him!**

My Sister's Healing

My sister's healing was one of the greatest miracles that I have ever seen in all my life. It was the greatest instant miracle I ever saw Jesus perform.

My sister was the first person I ever led to the Lord Jesus. She used to go frequently to nightclubs, just as I had. God began to deal with me on my way home from a nightclub one night and I got saved. I began to go to church and read the Bible. I didn't witness much to my family because I felt like they would make fun of me. Before I was saved we had all gone out together every Saturday night.

One Saturday night after supper, I got out my Bible, went to the table and began to read it. Mary, four years older than I am, was getting ready to go to the nightclub. She saw me sitting there and said, "John, why don't you go out any more?" I thought, "Well, she's going to make fun of me now." I turned to her and said, "Mary, I will just be honest with you. I have given my heart to Jesus. (I was ready for her to make fun of me.) And I am through with the nightclub circuit. I have found Jesus as my Saviour."

I just bowed my head waiting for her to make fun of me. When I looked up, she was crying. She said, "John, do you think Jesus would save anybody like me?" I said, "Mary, I know He will." She knelt down right beside me at that table and gave her heart to Jesus.

She joined a good Baptist church and served God faithfully. Many years went by. She was dedicated to God and serving Jesus with all of her heart. She taught a Baptist Sunday school class that had to be divided again and again because it would grow so large. She was a wonderful soul winner. After many years of living for God, the devil attacked her whole being. She suddenly was stricken with something like epilepsy. It got worse, and worse, and worse. I don't have words to describe the torment she suffered.* Actually, she lost her physical health, her mental health and her emotional health. She had violent attacks.

She said, "It seemed like I was sucked down into a deep dark hole. I could feel myself being sucked down into the darkness. My memory began to go. Finally I couldn't even remember the many scriptures that I had memorized. I cried out in anguish just trying to remember the Name of God."

She had to have twenty-four hour nursing care every day. She could not feed herself. She could not walk. She had to lie there in bed with nursing care twenty-four hours a day.

She said, "I knew that if I could just remember the Name of God I could keep my sanity. I could see the demon forces in my room. I could hear demon forces in my room. One day I just felt myself being pulled down into the deep part of that pit. Then suddenly I could not even remember the Name of God." She prayed to die and be free of the seizures and the demonic torment.

I had heard she was sick. While driving down the freeway, my sister, Mary, had been brought before me in a vision. My wife, mother-in-law and children were in the car with me. I said, "I haven't

*Mary Given's testimony in her own words is recounted in the book *You Can Change Your Destiny* by John Osteen.

heard about Mary but I know she is in bad shape. God is telling me that the hour of her deliverance has come."

Mary told me a very strange thing happened to her. One day she had one of the most violent attacks. She said that out of her innermost being there came a voice (no doubt it was God speaking to her), and it said, "Call John. Call John. Call John." She knew God meant me, her brother, John.

Thank God for His mercy. At this time my wife was expecting a baby. Soon after the revelation from the Lord, my mother called me and said, "Oh John, Mary is so sick." She wept as she told me how bad she was. Then she said, "When can you come? When can you come?" I said, "Mother, we are expecting our baby. As soon as she is born, I will come."

If you will just keep loving your family, then one day they will ask you to come.

Our baby was born the next day. I got in my car and drove all the way to Dallas. I had a 240-mile prayer meeting! I prayed a 240-mile prayer.

While I was praying in tongues, I could imagine little old demon forces sitting on the hood of my car, one on top, one on the rear, and one on the bumper. One would say, "What's he talking about?" Another says, "I don't know. I can't understand that language."

Thank God, we speak secrets to God. I Corinthians 14:2: "For he that speaketh in an unknown tongue speaketh not unto men, but unto God: For no man understandeth him; howbeit in the spirit he speaketh mysteries."

When I arrived in Dallas, I asked Brother H.C. Noah, an Assembly of God pastor, if he would go with me and he said he would. We went to Mary's house. The Presbyterian nurse came to the door. We went inside. I felt the anointing of God. I felt like I was twenty-five feet tall. I thank God you don't *have to feel* the anointing, but feeling is good. The nurse escorted us into the back bedroom. It was all dark in there, and there lay my precious sister. Her hair was matted. Her eyes were glassy. Her face was swollen. I wouldn't have recognized my own sister on the streets of Dallas.

Oh, I hate the devil!

When I went by in that darkened room, my sister put out her hand and mumbled, "Ahhhhhh," just like a groan. I had not known that she could not walk. I did not know about the terrible attacks she had been going through. Even as I tell this story, I remember vividly how bad she looked then. Do you know what I felt? It wasn't joy. It wasn't sympathy.

It was anger! An holy anger swept over me.

I have only felt that way a few times in my life. I remember that I walked over to the window, grabbed the drapery cord and I pulled it open. I said, **"God is light, let light in here!"** I went to the other window and did the same thing. I said, **"God is light, let light in here!"**

Then, looking at my sister, I said, **"Don't tell me God did this to my sister!"**

The Presbyterian nurse ran out!

Brother Noah and I stood over my sister. I said, "Mary, in the Name of the Lord Jesus Christ, I command the devil and every demon force to leave you and to leave this room and to leave this house. In the Name of the Lord Jesus Christ, rise and walk. Be free and healed in Jesus' Name!"

You see, I didn't know she couldn't walk. Suddenly it looked like four people took her and threw her against the wall. Her body was hurled across the room. Then she fell down in a little heap just like a dishrag.

Brother Noah and I took her and stood her up. I didn't know she hadn't walked in weeks. We put our hands on her and I began to pray in other tongues, forgetting that she was a Baptist. Suddenly I heard myself saying, "Receive ye the Holy

Ghost." Mary raised her hands and began to speak in other tongues!

That very moment she ran through that house completely well. Her sanity returned. And she ran through that house rejoicing and praising God.

That day she went to the table and fed herself. That day she gave up her Dilantin tablets. That has been many, many years ago, and she is still healed today. Thank God for the power of Jesus' Name!

Later she told me this, "John, first of all I remember when you came in the door and I heard somebody saying, 'Don't tell me God did this to my sister.'" She said, "Did you know I had a lingering thought that maybe I was suffering for Jesus, and that this affliction was the will of God? When somebody said that, I said to myself, 'Well maybe it isn't the will of God for me to be this way.'" She said, "Then I remember how I was liberated. It was when I heard somebody talking in a language I couldn't understand. That language went through my mind and echoed deep down on the inside of me. It broke the evil power. It broke through the darkness. It liberated me completely. It began to lift me out of that pit."

She said, "I'll tell you I heard Almighty God say,

'Mary, rise and walk.'" I said, "No Mary, I said it. You heard me say it." She insisted, "I heard Almighty God say 'rise and walk.'" I said, "No Mary, you heard me say it. I said it. I was standing there. I said it." She said, "Don't tell me what I heard! I heard a resounding, majestic voice, the Ancient of Days, and it came out of heaven and it said **'rise and walk!'"**

You see, when we walk in God, when we move in the Holy Ghost and speak in the Holy Ghost, our voice is blended with the voice of God.

For days after Mary was healed, I stayed there and taught her the Word of God. She has stayed in the Word of God day and night continually all these years.

Sixteen years after she had received her healing, every symptom came back on her body. Satan said, **"I will return!"** I hear his foul voice speak. "I will devour. I will steal. I will kill. I will destroy."

Kenneth Copeland heard me tell this story of my sister's healing and he asked me, "Brother Osteen, do you realize what happened? She had so much Word in her, it took the devil sixteen years to get up enough nerve to come back!"

Sixteen years after her healing, every symptom came back. She called me. I said, "I will be there as soon as I can. I will catch a plane right away." So, like I did before, I went right to her. I went to her home and tried to minister to her. Nothing happened. Nothing happened!

She said, "John, it's not up to you now. In the realm of understanding healing, I was a baby Christian before. I did not know about healing and God had mercy on me." (How many of you know that you got healed when you were first a Christian easier than you do now? God expects more out of you now.) She said, "You go on back home. You are not going to be able to do it for me. I am going to have to do it myself. I am going to hold fast to my confession of healing. I am going to have to hold fast to what I already have."

She rose up in her authority in Christ, took the Word of God, and spoke to the devil. She drove him out in the Name of Jesus. Today she is perfectly well!

God tells you to *hold fast* to what you *already have*. *Hold fast* to your *confession*. Don't ever change what you are saying. Say what God says about you. It does not matter if every symptom of financial distress, mental disorder, emotional upset or physical disease comes. *Hold fast* to your confession.

The devil said, "I will return. I will steal, kill and destroy. And I will devour."

I say, "Devil, you can try but you are not going

to do it in my house. No, you are not going to do it in my house. The devil cannot do his work in my house." Somebody asked me, "Aren't you afraid the devil will hear you?" I want him to hear me!

I want to give the devil a nervous breakdown. I want to keep him on tranquilizers! Every morning when I wake up, he looks and says, "Oh, no, he's awake again."

I want him to know that I boldly say that he cannot put disease on us. He cannot destroy us. He cannot steal from us. We will hold fast to that which God has given us!! We hold fast to our confession of the Word of God.

When the devil comes to you and says, "I will return. I will devour. I will steal, kill and destroy," what are you going to do? Will you roll over like my dog, Scooter? Will you just lie down and say, "I give up"? Will you accept defeat just because a little old hairy stinking demon came around and barked at you? Is that what you are going to do? Or are you going to act like the mighty sons and daughters of God? It is not up to you to find some great man or woman of God, or anybody else to pray for you. When the going gets tough, the tough get going!

You need to know the Bible yourself. You need to find out who you are in Christ. You need to know how to stand your ground! **You** need to do it **yourself!**

I put notes all over my house that remind me of God's promises. I boldly make my confession. I boldly declare my place in Christ.

You need to know four things. You need to know who Christ is. You need to know what Christ has done for you. You need to know who you are in Christ. And you need to know what you can do in the power of the Name of Jesus.

If you remain ignorant and lazy and unwilling to learn, if you make fun of faith teaching and Bible teachings and go along with shallow denominationalism, if you turn your back on Bible principles, then I guarantee you that when the devil comes you will not be ready for him. You will be no match for him! Why? Because you have made fun of the very thing that will set you free.

Boldly make this confession:
I know who I am in Christ!
I know what I can do in Christ!
I bear the Name of Jesus!
I am washed by the Blood of Jesus!
I am in the family of God!
I have the life of God in me!
I am filled with the Spirit of God!
I am in the kingdom of God!

In Jesus' Name I cast out demons!

I resist the devil and he flees from me!

The devil is on the run!

In your spiritual life, I want you to stand up tall. Do not murmur like the Israelites, for many of them were destroyed. There is always something destroyed when you murmur. Quit murmuring! Quit complaining! Quit being weak. Learn who you are in God. "If thou canst believe, all things are possible to him that believeth" (Mark 9:23).

Your greatest dream, your highest aspirations can come true. Some of you may be thinking, "You are talking about holding on to it when you get it, but I don't even have it yet!" Yes, you do! All the blessings of God are already yours. Jesus already died and rose again to give you all of God's blessings.

Salvation and healing have already been provided in the redemptive work of the Cross. All you need is to find the scriptures that pertain to your situation and believe them. You could have been **healed a long time ago** if only you had known about it and believed God for it!

Say what God says about you. Make these confessions about yourself:

I am of God (I John 4:4).

I have overcome the evil one (I John 4:4).

Greater is He that is in me, than he that is in the world (I John 4:4).

Christ has redeemed me from the curse of the law (Galatians 3:13).

I am living in the blessings of Abraham (Galatians 3:14).

I am blessed.

I am blessed in the city. I am blessed in the field (Deuteronomy 28:3).

I am blessed when I go out. I am blessed when I come in (Deuteronomy 28:6).

I know who I am in Christ.

I bear the Name of Jesus.

Satan will not steal one thing that God has given me (John 10:10).

I stand my ground.

Having done all, I stand (Ephesians 6:13).

I am strong in the Lord and the power of His might (Ephesians 6:10).

I have on the whole armour of God (Ephesians 6:11).

I am able to stand against all the wiles and all the strategies of the devil (Ephesians 6:11).

I am more than a conqueror (Romans 8:37).

I am not a weakling.

I am not like that dog that gave up.

I will not give up.

I will not be ashamed of Jesus or His Word (Romans 1:16).

I will stand tall!!

I will bear the Name that is above every name, the Name of Jesus (Philippians 2:9-10).

I will take my stand and my place as a child of God.

I will drive the enemy from the field of battle (James 4:7).

I stand as more than a conqueror (Romans 8:37).

Healing is mine (I Peter 2:24).

Health is mine (III John 2).

Prosperity is mine (Deuteronomy 28:8, 12).

The blessing of God is mine (Galatians 3:14).

All my needs have been supplied. I will begin to act like it (Philippians 4:19).

God's blessings are mine today! The devil will not rob me.

I will keep what God has given me! (Revelation 2:25)

Order additional materials from:

Lakewood Church
P.O. Box 23297
Houston, TX 77228

Copyright © 1980 John Osteen